Communicate!

How You Say It

Dona Herweck Rice

Publishing Credits

Rachelle Cracchiolo, *M.S.Ed., Publisher*
Conni Medina, *M.A.Ed., Managing Editor*
Nika Fabienke, *Ed.D., Series Developer*
June Kikuchi, *Content Director*
John Leach, *Assistant Editor*
Kevin Pham, *Graphic Designer*

Image Credits: All images from iStock and/or Shutterstock.

Library of Congress Cataloging-in-Publication Data

Names: Rice, Dona, author.
Title: Communicate! : How you say it / Dona Herweck Rice.
Description: Huntington Beach, CA : Teacher Created Materials, [2017] | Series: Time for kids
Identifiers: LCCN 2017026883 (print) | LCCN 2017029754 (ebook) | ISBN 9781425853310 (eBook) | ISBN 9781425849573 (pbk.)
Subjects: LCSH: Communication--Juvenile literature.
Classification: LCC P91.2 (ebook) | LCC P91.2 .R43 2017 (print) | DDC 302.2--dc23
LC record available at https://lccn.loc.gov/2017026883

Teacher Created Materials
5301 Oceanus Drive
Huntington Beach, CA 92649-1030
http://www.tcmpub.com

ISBN 978-1-4258-4957-3

Printed by: 51497
Printed in: China

What is the best way to say something?
The right words depend on where you are.
They also depend on who is around you.

What if something does not make sense?

With friends you may say,
"I don't get it."
With your teacher you
may say, "I do not
understand."

What if you **dislike** a strange food you just tasted?

With friends you may say, "Yuck!"
With your family you may say, "I do not care for this."

What if you are running late?

With friends you may say, "Come on!" With your father you may say, "We should go now."

What if something new makes you happy?

With friends you may say, "How cool!"
With your teacher you may say, "That is really great!"

What if you need to use the restroom?

At home you may say, "I really have to go!" With your teacher you may ask, "May I please use the restroom?"

What if something makes you frustrated?

With friends you may say, "Help!"
With your mother you may say, "Please help me."

What if you see someone laugh as they look at a computer screen?

With friends you may say, "Let me see!"
With your father you may ask, "May I look?"

What if you do not hear what someone said?

With friends you may ask, "What?"
With your teacher you may ask, "Will you please repeat that?"

What if you meet someone for the first time?

You may say, "Hi," when the person is your age. When you meet an **adult**, you may say, "It is nice to meet you."

You can choose the right words each time you speak.

That is your word superpower!

Glossary

adult

dislike

frustrated

screen